Overheard at the Dance

Adapted from the musical
The Dance

Book and lyrics by
Carol Lynn Pearson

Music by JAC Redford

Overheard at the Dance

Carol Lynn Pearson

Bookcraft
Salt Lake City, Utah

Library of Congress Catalog Card Number: 81-67067
ISBN O-88494-427-1

First Printing, 1981

Lithographed in the United States of America
PUBLISHERS PRESS
Salt Lake City, Utah

They
come
to the
dance.

The hopeful, the desperate, the assigned, the dating, the married. They have transformed the cultural hall into a heaven of crepe paper clouds and silver stars and rainbow streamers and (although the budget can't afford it) one of those balls that has hundreds of mirrors that throw little bits of the celestial all over the dancers.

They've worked hard since early morning—the girls wearing T-shirts and jeans and curlers and rolls of masking tape; and the boys, who like to carry heavy things, especially if the girls are nearby to notice. So they staple and hang and giggle and wrestle and send out to McDonald's for food. And finally they rest from their labors and look at their little heaven and call it good. Well, there are still some spots in the false ceiling that are a little skimpy, but the lights are going to be low anyway.

So they go home to shower off the sweat and put on the after-shave (many after not even shaving) and take out the curlers and put on the hair spray and the base and the eye shadow and the mascara and the lipstick and the perfume and the dress that finally passed kitchen correlation after a little piece was added to the neckline.

They come to the dance because it is not good for man to be alone. And certainly not for woman to be alone. And at the dance there is the sensation, or at least the possibility, of being *with* somebody. They can present themselves to be examined and admired and fallen in love with.

That's what it comes down to. Love. Not exactly the love they've been giving two-and-a-half-minute talks on since they were six. Not the "love thy neighbor as thyself" kind of love, although there is that too. The boys will tell the girls they look nice even if they think they're real dogs, because that's the golden rule. And the girls won't turn down a boy they can't stand, because of the "inasmuch as ye have done it unto the least of these" factor. (Unless they can avoid him by going to the ladies' room, in which case it doesn't count toward rudeness.)

But that's not the kind of love that brings them here. Not agape, that pure and unconditional love they talk about in Sunday School. What was the other kind? It was on the board in seminary. Eros? That's it. The word is a little too close for comfort to the name of the adult newspaper place right next door to the Kirby vacuum shop that was shut down last year. (The adult newspaper place was shut down, not the Kirby vacuum shop. Kirby vacuums are clean, *really* clean.)

So let's don't call it eros. Let's just call it being in love as opposed to just plain love. Romantic love. That's why they come to the dance. It's a being in love kind of place. It's warm and soft and musical and dim, and the opposite sex is there in great numbers, and you can touch them and it's okay, and there's something about the bright little bits from the mirrored ball that makes you think of time and all eternity. Or is it that great after-shave? Or the warm hand on your back? Well, something makes you think of time and all eternity, and it feels really nice.

Everybody acts cool about it. Cool and casual, as if they were not about the most profound of human business, a most godly business, the reaching of male and female for each other. They are beings that are already whole and yet in their wholeness have mystically become a part of an even greater whole and yearn for the completion. So they bring their yearning to the ritual of the dance and exercise it over the punch bowl and between dances and during dances. And they act cool. Cool and casual.

Would the owner of the blue Lincoln, license number DKJ-417, please go out and turn out the lights? The couple in the car in front are complaining. Just joking. I'm your MC tonight. Again. When they asked me I said, 'Why don't you ask Brother Halverson? He'd be a great MC.' They said, 'We had him, and when he finished all his jokes we had to rededicate the cultural hall.' Just joking, of course. I guarantee all my jokes will be as pure as the driven snow. They could all be printed in the *Reader's Digest*. In fact, most of them *have* been. Enough of this chit-chat. You didn't come to hear me. Let's dance!"

That's Howard. You know him. Everybody knows him. The eternal bachelor. Witty. Poised. Guarded. Everybody knows him. And nobody knows him.

"You're really a good dancer," he says to Alison, the young woman he met at the stake special interest fireside last week. "For a person who's as out of practice as you say you are, you're really very good."

Howard is considering getting a toupee, it's such a bother to comb his hair over the thin place. Maybe if he went away for the summer and came back with a toupee nobody would notice.

"Oh, I dance with my babies," replies Alison. "I always have. I put on some good music and pick them up and away we go. But dancing with a man is—different."

"We're—bigger, huh?"

"Yes. And—uh—different."

"You have three?" Howard always smiles a little more than necessary when asking about his date's children.

"Yes." Alison brightens. "You like children?"

"Sure. I even used to be one." They both laugh. Laughter comes easily at the dance. It's just *there*, with the crepe paper and the band.

"Uh, listen." Howard lowers his voice a little. "Because this is your first date since . . . since you've been dating . . . I think I'd be doing you a favor to tell you something. You don't say to a guy, 'Do you like children?' Most men would take it as a very . . . leading question."

"I—I can see that. Thanks." It's not easy to discover all the do's and don'ts of her new role. Like whether to leave her left hand out in plain sight or whether to keep it hidden. It still feels bare without the rings, sometimes cold, even.

"You want to keep things light," Howard continues. "Tell a funny story. Got any funny stories?"

"Well, yesterday my little Bobby—Oh! It's about my child." She would never get the hang of it.

"That's okay. Just keep it light."

"Well, Bobby came back from washing his hands in ten seconds flat and I said, 'Bobby, don't tell me you washed your hands.' And he said, 'I don't use soap, Mommy. I just drown the germs and wipe them off.' "

"That's good." Howard nods. "That's very funny."

"Bobby's clever. You would like him. Oh!"

Alison gives Howard an apologetic little smile. He shrugs and smiles back. They dance.

5

Adolescent love energy is almost palpable, even in the chapel when it's trying for reverence. And here in the cultural hall-turned-heaven, with the after-shave and the perfume and that incredible mirrored ball and the sound of the band, it is so thick it hits you in waves. It's the potent, confused kind of energy that supposedly attracts poltergeists. At least it attracts other adolescents. Anywhere. Especially at the dance.

Brad is full of it, pulsing with it. Eros coupled with agape is many years down the road. Right now it's eros coupled with hate. The object of his energy is Marcie, the blonde at the punch bowl in the dress that clearly did not have to go through kitchen correlation. She shot him down just last week. That's why he is here with Janet, his brother's old girl friend.

"Turn around! Don't let her see you staring at her," Brad whispers loudly, jerking Janet by the elbow.

"Look at that dress," exclaims Janet, craning her neck to see. "How old did you say she is?"

"Seventeen."

"She'll grow up," comforts Janet. "Take it from an old woman of twenty-three."

"Shhhhhh!" Brad's hand quickly covers her mouth. "I don't want anyone to know."

"That I'm—"

"An old woman."

"Hey, *I* can say that. You can't. So I'm five years older than you are."

"Shhhhhhh!" Brad's eyes dart around. The couple dancing beside them are laughing. At him? No, he guesses

6

not. "If the guys found out, they'd razz me for a year. But I had to come. I had to show her she isn't the only girl in the world."

"I will put on the show of the year." Janet runs her fingers up his arm and around his shoulder. "I will fawn on you, my dear, all evening." She wraps her arms around him. "Oh, Brad, you are so irresistible!"

"Cut it out!" Brad whispers through clenched teeth, grabbing her wrists and pulling them down. "Good grief!—look what happens to that dress when she walks. Good grief!"

Janet covers his eyes with her hand. "Don't look, Brad. You're too young."

"Why would she *do* that?" Brad's eyes are riveted.

"She does it because *she* thinks that *he* thinks that that's the way he would like her to be. And maybe even *he* thinks that that's what he would like. But *I* think that he thinks that she thinks that that's what she is, but really is not. Don't you think so?"

"Uh, yeah." Brad shakes his head, closes his eyes, and leads Janet in the other direction.

"Most girls fall into that trap at one point or another," Janet continues.

"You didn't. You were always . . . just you."

"Oh, but you didn't know me at age nineteen. That was my worst. You would not believe all the really dumb, stupid, outrageous things I would do to be what I thought this guy wanted, or that guy wanted. Just so somebody would *love* me."

"Yeah?"

"For instance, Fred said he wanted a real domestic

goddess, right? 'Oh, sure,' I said. 'Maintaining a home in domestic bliss is all I ask of life.' So I worked on it. Crocheting. Quilting. On the day he introduced me to his mother, she was just finishing canning her eight hundred forty-fourth quart of fruit for the summer, and that didn't even count tomatoes and jam. She asked me if I used the pressure cooker or the water bath, and I said, 'Well, personally I prefer to shower.' She did not think that was funny. And later that night—Fred did not propose."

Brad laughs. "Good thing. Somehow I don't think canning is the real you."

"And for Milt, who wanted a soft, sweet, demure, feminine creature, I became one. Or tried. But then, after we had seen this certain movie, he said, 'That was the best movie I've seen in years. Wasn't that great?' And I shyly said, 'No, I don't think it was great at all. I thought the plot was flawed and the characters were terribly one-dimensional, and the theme was handled much better by Fellini.' And—Milt sent me a postcard the next year from school."

"Terrific!" Brad observes. "Demure you are not."

"But I tried. I really tried. And then there was Ron. For him I was going to swim and ski and get up at five and jog. Well, one day while my leg was mending, Dad came up to my room and said, 'Why do you do this? If you want to know who you ought to be, why don't you ask yourself? After all, you are a person, you know.' Me, a person? Well, what did I have to lose? So I asked myself how I wanted to cut my hair, what I wanted to read, where I wanted to go, what I wanted to do. Then I listened. And I learned some

8

things. I like waterbeds. I like almond fudge. I do not think the government should pay people not to grow food. I like reading to old people in rest homes. I like sleeping in. I hate red lipstick. I am not interested in skiing. I might like to put up pickles, but nix on eight hundred forty-four bottles of fruit every summer. I love John Denver and Liza Minelli. I like wearing Levi's every day except Sunday. So you see, Brad, the moral of the story is that fitting into what somebody wants you to be really does make them love you."

"Yeah?" Brad asks.

"Well, I love me. I think I'm terrific."

"How about some punch?" Brad leads in the direction of the punch bowl.

"I *hate* lime punch," says Janet. "But for *you*, Brad . . ."

The love energy of the ten years married is considerably different from that of the adolescent. Sometimes eros goes on vacation for long periods of time, leaving agape coupled with agape, or even sometimes agape coupled with irritation or restlessness or a vague disappointment.

"Decorations are great, huh?" Neil waits a moment for Karen to speak. She doesn't. The band is finally playing a tune for them instead of for the teenagers. "Blue moon, you saw me standing alone." Alone. That's what you get married for—so you won't be alone. But sometimes you can be alone even when you're married, even when you're dancing with your own wife.

Neil tries again. "Looks like a pretty good turnout." Still nothing. He takes a deep breath. "Well, I hate to let this time go to waste. So—uh, I'm thankful for my wife. She's the lady here who's not speaking to me."

Karen's hands drop to her side and her feet stop moving. "Neil. You are being sacrilegious."

"Well, you're being mean. And that's worse."

"Can we sit this one out?"

"Sure." Neil makes his way to the folding chairs and Karen follows. They look at the dancers. And their hands. And the celestial ball that turns and turns.

"Why the stony silence?"

"We didn't used to have to talk at a dance," Karen replies. "We could spend a whole evening and hardly say a word."

"There is a difference between a warm, companionable silence and an icy chill. Like about one hundred degrees. What did I do? What did I say?"

"Nothing."

The tune was just finishing. " . . . Now I'm no longer alone. . . ."

"Nothing," Neil echoes. Then he turns to the empty folding chair beside him. "And one of the qualities I most appreciate in my wife is her candid frankness. Now, what-

10

ever is going on here seems to have started late this afternoon. We have to give a workshop, see, at this marriage enrichment seminar—"

Karen looks straight ahead. "Neil, will you stop it?"

"All I did was suggest a title for our session. We have to have a title."

"Right. 'Is There Life After Marriage?' "

"It's funny, Karen. It's a funny title."

Karen slides onto the folding chair on the other side, leaving a chair between her and her husband.

"The way you said it was *not* funny! And the answer to the question is not funny either!" She is expecting Neil to slide over beside her. He doesn't.

"Whoa! What's your answer?"

Karen pauses a moment and puts her hand on the chair between them, her palm feeling the cold metal. "No. There isn't. Not like there's supposed to be. Not like there was going to be."

Neil is supposed to reach over and take the hand that is on the chair between them. He doesn't. All he does is lean back and fold his arms and say, "Oh! Where do you want me to put the body?"

Karen waves her hand at the empty chair. " 'It has been clinically established, after a great deal of testing, that there is not life after marriage.' That's what we should say at the seminar? That's real faith-promoting!"

Neil does not speak. He just rocks on the back legs of the folding chair the way his mother always told him not to and the way that Karen sometimes reminds him about at home.

"Neil, we used to be in love! We used to come to these

11

dances and be in ecstacy just to be able to put our arms around each other. Don't you remember?"

"I remember."

"And it's different now. Haven't you noticed?"

"I've noticed." Neil continues to rock. "Your pulse doesn't go up at all anymore."

"What?"

"You know how I could tell you were in love with me? A little trick I learned first year of medical school. I took your pulse while I was kissing you."

"You didn't!"

"I did that to all the girls I kissed. I'd keep one hand on her wrist, or, if I could, right here on the throat. Let me show you."

"Don't touch me!" There are now two folding chairs between them.

"Do you remember the first time I kissed you? You went right off the chart."

"You are disgusting!" Karen turns away and puts a hand over her eyes.

Neil stops rocking. "You don't go off the chart anymore. You don't go anywhere."

Karen whirls back to him. "You see? What did I tell you? I'm dead! *We're* dead!"

"Hey, come on now, Karen." Neil moves into the nearest of the two chairs between them. "We're in this thing forever."

"Thanks, Neil. That's a real comfort."

Neil's hand reaches for her face and turns it toward him. Their eyes meet for the first time since lunch. "You want to give it up?"

"No! I . . ." Her eyes break away and fasten on the celestial ball. "I don't know what I want."

"We knew what we were getting into." Neil puts a hand on her shoulder. "Time and all eternity."

"The eternity part does not bother me." Karen's eyes go from the celestial ball back to her hands. "It's the time part that I'm getting worried about."

"Hey, there's another great title—'The Eternity Part Does Not Bother Me—It's the Time Part—' "

Karen interrupts. "Neil, we don't have *time* for the funnies."

"Why?"

Karen looks at him and then back at her hands. "I have to call Lonnie before ten-thirty and give her the title, plus a summary of what we're going to be saying."

"What?" The front legs of Neil's chair hit the floor with a thud.

"She has to type it for the announcement sheet. We were supposed to get it to her by Thursday. But that was the day the kids got sick, and then the next day—"

"Skip it." Neil looks at his watch and slides over beside her. "Okay. We've got an hour and fifteen minutes. Let's get this meeting underway. Oh, boy! I thought I was taking my wife out to the dance—and it turns into *another lousy meeting!*" He sits erect, hands on knees, elbows out, and speaks loudly. "All right—who has the spiritual thought?"

"Shhhhh!" Karen responds with a violent whisper. "Not me!"

They look at the dancers. And their hands. And the celestial ball that turns and turns.

13

In a moment Neil rocks back on his chair. "Can this marriage be saved? Let alone exalted."

Karen turns to him. "And you did *not* just come to take your wife out to the dance. You came to chaperone. We are here because *you* were *assigned* to be here. And before long you'll be having more Daddy-Daughter dates than dates with your wife. And we did *not* know what we were getting into. Nobody does. Ever."

Some teenagers dance by, locked in embrace. Karen looks at them and shakes her head. They have no idea. None. When you're young it seems so simple. You fall in love. You do everything perfectly. The bishop even uses you as an example in his annual "Meet Your Mate at Church" talk. You get married and you're supposed to live happily ever, ever, ever after. Only sometimes . . . you look across the table or the bed and you say, "What am I doing with this *person?*" A god in embryo who chews with his mouth open.

Neil slowly stands and opens his arms to her, and they dance. Sometimes dancing is good because you don't have to look at each other. And the band is playing another one for them. "They asked me how I knew my true love was true. . . ." How does anyone know anything about love? How did that wonderful beginning deliver something so ordinary—so trying, even? How do you *will* romance? When they had been engaged they had laughed together over that magazine article that claimed it took an average of seven months for passion to turn to compassion. But here he is, signed, sealed and delivered into eternity with a good woman who has halitosis in the morning and large pores on her nose. Does this really go

14

on forever? Even conference has a closing prayer. What was that Peggy Lee song?—"Is That All There Is?" They don't look at each other. And they dance.

"You're pretty quiet, Alison."

"Oh!" Alison looks up with a quick smile. "I'm just trying to think of some more funny stories."

"Relax. Just relax."

"I'll try." Alison looks around at the other dancers. Some of them are relaxed. Others are trying. Real hard. How do you *try* to relax? Isn't that a contradiction in terms? There's those exercises her mother had sent her when she couldn't sleep, tightening each muscle at a time and then letting go. She doesn't think it would work on the dance floor.

"You having fun?" Howard asks.

"Yeah. Sure. It's just—a very strange thing, you know, to be out on a date. Just having to make conversation with a man over seven . . . makes me nervous."

"You're cute. Just say whatever happens to come to your mind."

"Howard." Alison looks him straight in the eyes the way she does with her children when she has something important to say. "People *never* do that. I should go up to somebody and say, 'Hi, I'm Alison, and I just got a divorce, and I still cry at least once a day, and I don't even like to go to church anymore because all of a sudden I'm not a person, I'm a problem.' That's what I should say?"

Howard narrows his eyes and nods. "You're right. Think of another funny story. Tell you what, Alison. You've got to have your answers all ready, a whole list of them. Somebody asks what happened to your marriage, and you say, oh, . . . 'It's better to have loved and lost. Much better.' "

Alison pauses a moment, her eyes still fixed on him. "Really?"

"Sure. You can't just come out and suffer in front of people. It makes them terribly . . . uncomfortable."

"I know."

"Take me, for example," Howard goes on. "Sure, I'd like to be married, have a nice little wife and family. But I can't make a big tragic deal out of it. Ask me why I'm not married. Go ahead. I get it at least three times a week. Ask me."

Alison gives a short sigh, like she does with her children when they insist she drop the vitamins into their mouths while they're on the floor instead of just taking them like normal people. "Howard, why aren't you married?"

"My intended mate was killed in the war in heaven."

"That's old." Alison laughs and shakes her head. "That was going around when I was in college."

"Yeah? Ask me again."

Another short sigh. "Howard, why aren't you married?"

"It's not my fault I'm single. I was born this way."

Alison laughs. "Oh, Howard!" Someone looking at her would definitely say she's one of the relaxed, not one of the trying.

Howard is in good form now. "Tell me I'm going to end up a ministering angel."

No sigh. "You're going to end up a ministering angel, Howard."

Howard strikes a pose, finger in air. "Service above self! That's a good one, huh?"

Alison laughs again and it feels easy. She looks at Howard, beaming. He loves to make people laugh. Sort of like—oh, forget the children! Children are not allowed at the dance. Just men. Because they're . . . bigger. And different. They really are different.

There are about thirty used punch cups on the tray waiting to go back to the kitchen. About ten of them have lipstick on them. Brad stares at them. One of the cups with lipstick is Marcie's. If he knew which one he'd smile and throw it on the floor and watch it shatter, even if it was bought with money from the ward budget.

"Do you want to tell me about your big romance, or is it too painful?"

Brad's eyes slowly leave the punch cups. "You won't laugh?"

"Of course not. You know all about my big romance with Jay. You even hid behind the couch one night when he brought me over to watch TV."

"Okay. Well, I was never much interested in girls. Always had better things to do. Then, three weeks ago, it happened."

Janet raises her hands as if to play the violin and begins to hum.

"You said you wouldn't laugh."

Janet puts down the violin and leans back on the table. "I'm not laughing. I'm bleeding. It's too familiar."

"It couldn't have happened to you like this. It's never happened to anybody like this."

"I'd better sit down for this one."

Brad and Janet leave the table, the punch cups with lipstick that are still waiting to go back to the kitchen, and find two chairs in the corner.

"I'm ready." Janet leans forward, cupping her chin in her hands.

Brad looks up. The cups are just going into the kitchen.

"Well, I heard the guys talking about some new girl that had moved into the ward, but I didn't pay any attention. Then at roadshow rehearsal—I was walking toward the drinking fountain, and she was too, from the other way. We looked at each other. And suddenly it was like one of those shampoo commercials that go into slow motion, with people running through the fields. After about a hundred years we both got to the fountain at the same time, looking right in each other's eyes. Wow, those eyes! Blue, like . . . like the summer sky. Those eyes."

Janet nods. "Both of them."

Brad does not hear her. He is staring transfixed at the celestial ball and beyond it. "All these dumb things came into my mind to say. Like 'What are you doing for the next thousand years?' Or 'Didn't we meet in the preexistence?' But I just turned the handle of the fountain, real cool-like, and said, 'Can I buy you a drink?' After rehearsal she was waiting for me outside. I knew she would be. I walked her home, and it was all slow motion again."

"Her mother must have wondered why it took so long."

Brad still does not hear. He is way past the turning ball now. Way past. "I was in love. I couldn't sleep. I couldn't study. All I could think about was her. And those eyes."

Janet nods again. "Both of them."

"By that weekend, we'd planned our whole lifetime together. The kind of house we wanted. The names of our first six children. I told her I couldn't marry her until I could support her—there would be a mission, and college. She said, 'What's six years? I could wait forever for you.

You're the only one for me, Brad. I knew that for sure when I found those three roses in that vase on my window sill. A little voice inside me said this is the one I will love forever.' "

"How romantic."

Brad slams his fists down into his lap. He is back from the celestial ball now. Way back. "But I didn't give her any roses!"

"Oh, oh!"

"When I told her, she looked like I'd stabbed her in the stomach and said, 'I'm afraid I've made a terrible mistake.' "

"Who gave them to her?"

Brad points furiously across the hall. "*He* did! That's why she's with him tonight and not with me. Look at them! They're probably thinking up names for their first six children. They'd just better not use . . . Lisa—or Eric —or Kevin . . ." Brad gives a great sigh, tucks his hands into his armpits, and slumps down in the chair. He closes his eyes and speaks with controlled passion. "I sold my tape deck to buy her a promise ring!"

Janet puts a hand on his shaking knee. "Oh, Brad! I'm sorry! Keep it. Someday you'll use it."

"No! It'll never happen again. I trusted once. I loved once. And she threw me away like an old apple core. Never again!"

"Brad, you're only eighteen."

"What does age mean? My love life is over."

"Brad . . . take it from an old woman of twenty-three—"

"Shhhhhhhh!"

Janet stands and holds out her hand. "Let's dance."

Alison is relaxed now. There's something about moving your body to music and being with somebody who is good at telling funny stories that is relaxing. It even makes you a little bit bold.

"Howard," Alison ventures. "Can I ask you something?"

"Sure."

"I want a serious answer, now. Why aren't you married?"

Howard looks around, then speaks in a loud whisper. "Promise you won't tell?"

Alison nods.

"I've got terminal dandruff."

"Howard! Aren't you ever serious? Have you ever been engaged?"

"Only in a good cause. And the best cause I know of is staying single. Hey, that's really funny. I'll have to remember that one."

Alison shakes her head. "You're impossible!"

"Okay, I'll tell you the truth." Howard puts on the really earnest face he uses when he teaches the elders quorum. "I *do* want to get married. I know it's what I ought to do. And I *want* to. I've been working on it ever since I got back from my mission. Don't tell anybody, but my six months have been up twenty-eight times. That's fourteen years. I get tired of my mother introducing me as her son who never married. I get tired of her sending me newspaper clippings every time a jewelry store has a sale on diamonds. Two years ago I got so desperate that I . . . Okay! I heard somewhere how one of the Brethren met his wife. He decided it was time for him to get married, he fasted three days, prayed a lot, went to this certain place, and said to the Lord, 'Now the rest is up to you.' A girl came walking by, he started a conversation with her, and three weeks later they were married in the temple. Great story, huh?"

"Yeah. Great!"

"So I decided if it worked for him it would work for me. I fasted for three days, chose a good place. At first I was going to sit on the steps of the campus library at 6:00 A.M., but then I thought, What if she's working downtown or going to beauty school or something? I wanted to give everybody an equal chance. So at twelve noon on the big day I got on the bus downtown, and I said, 'Okay, Lord, you've had three days to arrange this. I'm going to close my eyes, and at the next bus stop, the first woman to get on is the one you want me to marry.' "

Alison stares at him in disbelief. "Oh, Howard!"

"So I closed my eyes. The bus stopped. I heard the

doors open and then close. I opened my eyes. And there was a sixty-five-year-old woman with a sack of groceries in her arms. She walked back and sat down right beside me, smiled, and said, 'Hello.' "

Alison covers her eyes. "And you said?"

"I took a deep breath, looked her in the eyes and said, 'Lady, I'm awfully hungry. Could you spare a slice of bread?' "

"Oh, Howard!" Alison laughs, the way you laugh at someone who has gotten exactly what he asked for. "You can't make bargains with the Lord. I just don't think he works that way."

"You're right." Howard does not laugh. He still has his elders quorum face on. "You can't tell the Lord the exact day and place to deliver her. You just have to keep your eyes open, have faith, and one day—there she'll be."

Cautiously Alison looks up to see if he's serious. He is. Faith is the key. He knows that. And he knows that very soon—just around the corner . . . or there across a crowded room . . . singing in the choir . . . or modestly making her way from the foyer into the chapel—will be her. Her. His girl. His eternal girl. He'll know her when he sees her. He'll recognize her by that special quality he's looking for. Perfection. She'll have her genealogy done way past four generations. She'll give the best little spiritual living lesson you've ever heard. She'll know all the verses to "Come, Come, Ye Saints," play the piano, dance, sing, paint. She'll be a very sought-after speaker at Young Women's standards nights, but she won't be a prude—she'll be warm, very warm, and at the right time and the right place seductive, even. And after they're married, what was perfection will blossom into absolute, unending, divine delight. He'll come home from work and there she'll be, canning her fruit while scripture cards are propped up on the table. Menus will be planned from a two-years' supply that's always up to date. She'll stay much more slim and trim than women who have less children than she has. A *lot* less. She'll do it by bicycling almost everywhere—to the grocery store, visiting teaching, PTA—with one or two wagons tied on behind in which the children sit contentedly eating small boxes of raisins. She'll be just what he's always dreamed of—sort of a nice combination of Miss America, his mother, and just a touch of Eliza R. Snow. Howard knows she's out there ... somewhere ... right this very minute—waiting for him to find her. It will be soon. She may even have a note from his bishop pinned to her dress—"This Is *The One!*" His girl. His sweetheart, helpmeet, baby-doll, queen. His eternal girl.

Hey, here's a great title." Neil is using his really enthusiastic voice, which works very well with small children and dubiously with adult women. " 'How to Stay Active in the Church by Going

Inactive in Your Marriage—or Ninety-Nine Approved Ways to Avoid Your Spouse.' "

"Neil, that is not fair!"

It's hard to carry on a conversation when you're not dancing in each other's arms—just sort of moving around in front of each other. Karen moves a little closer. "We don't avoid each other. At least, I don't avoid each other. And the Church takes less time than it used to. There's your job—and all of my involvements."

"So—they're all to blame. We're to blame. But somehow—in our marriage—we have slowly but surely dropped out of activity. And nobody has come by to see what's the matter. Not even us."

The band starts a new tune. If they want to they can stop moving around in front of each other and get a little closer. Or try. Karen moves her left hand up to his shoulder.

"But—but you have to make a living. Being an intern is tough."

"Sure. But you're as busy as I am. Three children . . . a house . . . school committee . . . church work. If ever I do have a minute, you don't. Sometimes I think you *do* stay busy just to avoid me."

"Neil, that's crazy!"

"Oh?"

"I'm *busy* because I've always been taught to *be* busy. Good little Mormon girls are taught you have to stay busy so the devil doesn't get you."

Neil sighs loudly. "Karen, I am not the devil. I am your husband. And once in a while I would *like* to *get* you. For instance, every time lately that I suggest retiring early for a

25

nice romantic experience, it just doesn't seem to work out. You've got to fold the laundry or make some calls for Relief Society. And when you do get time for me—I get the feeling it's sort of like compassionate service."

"That isn't fair, Neil! *I* plan a romantic experience every now and then."

"Once a month, like visiting teaching. 'Let me know if I can do anything else for you.' Do you call it in somewhere? 'Well, *he's* done.' "

Karen stares at him, her face frozen. Her voice lowers. "Neil! That was ugly."

Neil continues undaunted. Now that the worst is out it's easier. "I can live with it, Karen. I can live with it. But, look! I think I would feel better about it if you could get me at the first of the month instead of at the last."

Karen struggles with the muscles of her face for a moment and then surrenders to laughter. "Who could I call it in to? That's really a wonderful idea, Neil."

Neil shakes his head and looks up at the celestial ball. "Oh, boy!"

"Neil, guess what?"

"What?"

"I think you're right. I do avoid you. I mean, I think I . . . avoid talking about anything that's . . . difficult. *And* maybe I spend three times longer than I need to on my Relief Society lesson because—because I feel like I'm appreciated there. And on the school committee."

Neil speaks with his sincere voice. His unmistakably sincere voice. "Karen—you don't feel that I appreciate you?"

"Well, yes. But I don't think you really *see* me—like you used to see me. And I *need* that. I realize all the time how much I need that. At school they see me as 'Mrs.' At church they see me as 'Sister.' The children see me as 'Mother.' You see me as 'Wife.' But—way back behind all those people—there's somebody that I used to be, somebody that I need to be, somebody . . ."

Who? Where did she go? Why? If nobody ever speaks your name—your real name—you go inside and shut the door. But what is her real name? "Mother" is real. The person who brushes and braids the children's hair and makes the lunches and calls them all to evening prayer—she's real. And the wife who takes telephone messages and puts her hand on her husband's knee in sacrament meeting and folds his socks together the long way so it doesn't stretch the elastic—she's real. But—there's somebody else. The other day when she was trying to organize her files she began reading the letters she and Neil had written that summer they got engaged. She had started to cry. For a long time she just lay on the bed with the letters in her hand. If Neil had come home early she would not have been able to explain why she was crying. She couldn't even explain it to herself. Her five-year-old was the only one who saw her tears, and he thought she had probably just fallen down or something.

The girl she used to be—that's who's missing. The innocent, enthusiastic, desirable girl she used to be. She's graciously opened the territory to all these newer residents. But she feels pushed—evicted, even. And invisible. That's the worst part. Invisible.

Brad has been masterfully maneuvering over the dance floor in order to constantly be in a position where Marcie can see him without giving her the slightest hint that he can also see her. Or would even want to. Suddenly he whirls sharply and draws Janet in close. Really close. There! That should show Marcie she's not the only girl whose body feels nice up close! He whirls again and whispers in Janet's ear.

"She waved at me. Can you believe the nerve? She smiled and waved at me."

Janet pulls back to look around. Brad jerks her back in, not the way you do to somebody whose body feels nice up close. Sort of the way you do in an Indian arm wrestle.

"Don't look!"

Janet presses her cheek up against Brad's and whispers loudly, "Do you want to leave, Brad? I wouldn't mind if you want to."

"I can't."

"Why not?"

"I'm on the floor show."

"You didn't tell me."

"You didn't ask me."

"What's your act going to be—slitting your wrists?"

They have danced to the other end of the floor now and Brad relaxes his embrace, not tenderly like you do to someone whose body feels nice up close, but abruptly like you drop your tomahawk when the Indian scene is finished in the roadshow.

"Don't be dumb, Janet! I'm a tapper."

"You're kidding! A tap dance? Are you any good?"

28

"Good? I'm terrific! And when Marcie sees how terrific I am, boy, is she going to be sorry!"

"How long have you been dancing?"

"About a year. The basketball coach read somewhere that the top athletes take dance classes. Helps the foot-work—you know? So he enrolled us all in this class. It was just when Gene Kelly was coming back in. Did you see him do that number on roller skates?"

"Sure. It was great!"

"Anyway, I watched old Kelly up there tapping, and I thought, Wow, that looks more fun than making a basket! So—I stayed with the dance class and dropped the team."

"What'd the guys have to say about that?"

"Plenty. There's this one dude, Dan—called me Shirley Temple. Every time he saw me out in the parking lot he'd strut on over and say, 'Well, if it isn't Shirley Temple! Give us a dance, Shirley, huh?'"

"Oh, no!"

"At first I just keep right on walking. He catches up and says, 'Well, show me you're a man, Brad. Come on!' I try to think what a man ought to do in that situation. So I turn the other way. He slams his fist in my face and says, 'Be a man, Brad!' I remember in the Bible what it says you're supposed to do, so I turn the other cheek. He slams his fist into that side too. Well, I can't remember what the Bible says to do after that—so I beat the heck out of him. After my dance class I have a karate class. Anyway, I help him to the doctor to have him look at his head. Takes twelve stitches. I hold his hand and I say, 'Come on, Dan—be a man! Be a man!'"

When a girl laughs admiringly at your great stories and

29

the band plays a good tune, you can get this sense of well-being, of power. Brad dances his way through the crowd, living again his hour of triumph in the parking lot. The cheers of thousands ring in his ears. Wide shots of applauding fans fill the screen. And then a quick zoom-in on *her*, dancing with somebody that is not *him*. The cheers stop abruptly. The applauding fans look down in embarrassment. And Brad dances the other way.

Howard, what if she never makes her entrance like that? What if it never happens?" It's hard to choose words for a serious thought and make them sound not *too* serious. So Alison smiles as she says it, as if she's telling a joke. But she knows that she isn't.

"It'll happen." Howard's voice has the tone of a brief talk on faith. "And I'm not just waiting around. I'm working on it. I date at least twice a week. I'm always given the kind of church positions that force me into contact with women. Like I've been dance director about seven different times. All the bishops seem to think that if they can just keep me dancing, sooner or later one of my partners is bound to take."

"No wonder you're such a good dancer—all that practice! No wonder!"

"Yeah." Howard whirls her around masterfully. "It's like typing with your eyes closed. Hey, you know what dance was the first one I had to teach?"

"What?"

"The jitterbug."

"Oh, you're not that old."

"In my ward we got all the dances five years behind everybody else."

"Show me."

"The jitterbug?"

"Or some of the other ones. Can you remember?"

"Can I ever forget?" They are at the sidelines now. Howard plants himself and gestures to the passing dancers, who are handily there for his show and tell. "Here's this hall full of thirteen- to eighteen-year-olds, just dying to get their hands on each other. Right?"

"Right!"

"And I've got to teach them the dances and keep them moral at the same time. Right?"

"Right!"

"Every once in a while the bishop pops his head in to see if anybody needs to repent. Well, the jitterbug is not their favorite thing. The slow dances are their favorite because that's when they get to move in. And if they get too far in, then I have to take the floor and announce, 'Uh —the bishop says that he would prefer you not to dance cheek-to-cheek.' So it's back to the jitterbug. For a while, anyway."

"You must have seen a lot of different dances come and go."

"Have I ever! Listen! The last time I was dance director, the dances had gotten so outrageous—all those adolescent bodies were doing so many *strange* things—that I found myself announcing, 'Uh—the bishop says that he would prefer you to dance cheek-to-cheek.' "

Alison laughs. Howard draws her into his arms and they dance, cheek-to-cheek.

"I suppose I shouldn't say this, Howard." Alison pulls back an inch or two. "But it seems to me that you could dance with girls for the rest of your life and never really meet one."

"What do you mean?"

"I like your jokes, Howard. You're a very funny person. But I get the feeling there's a lot more to you than that. Only you don't want anybody to see it. Maybe you don't really want to meet anyone."

Howard looks at her. He wants to tell her she ought to go back to her funny stories. But there's something about the way she looks at him. Sort of open. And there's something about what she just said. Sort of true. He pulls her back in and they dance.

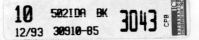

Neil looks at his watch. "Forty-five more minutes. Have we settled on 'I Changed My Mind—Where Is the Line for Ministering Angels?' With this description: 'Neil and Karen Bradley tell exactly how their celestial marriage has fallen in the mud and make embarrassing stabs at its revitalization.' "

"Cute, Neil."

"Well, then. 'Thirty-Seven Years With the Bradleys and Never a Harsh Word.' I like that. 'The inside story of a made-in-heaven marriage that gets sweeter and sweeter with each passing day. Listen and eat your heart out.' "

"We have only been married seven years."

"So? It isn't lying. It's—positive thinking. If you *pose* like the family on the cover of the *Ensign*, you're halfway there. Actually, Karen, I think we Mormons work very hard at putting up a good front. Regular, normal people out there in the world can admit they have problems. They're just human beings. Their marriages can have serious flaws. But not us Saints. We've got to hold up that *Ensign* cover because we're being *watched*. But you never really know what's going on inside."

Karen sighs, like you do when you hear something true that you don't want to agree with.

Neil goes on. "Do *you* do that, Karen?—work really hard to keep up the good front?"

Karen smiles, sweetly. "Why do you think we were asked to do the seminar?" And then sighs again. "Oh, boy! It all comes back to me. When we got married I was going to be your basic Model Mormon Wife and Mother—make all the children's clothes, bake everything from scratch, never ever raise my voice."

33

"I heard you raise your voice once," Neil objects.

"I also do not make all the children's clothes. Sometimes I don't even *wash* them all. Listen! Right in the middle of my worst bout with that fashionable disease called 'Mormon Women's Depression'—an occupational hazard named for us like writer's cramp, housemaid's knee, athlete's foot . . . 'Mormon Women's Depression'—low-grade fever, listlessness, rambling mutterings: 'Strike me again—I will be perfect, I will be perfect!'—"

"Hey! Hold it! I think I need to sit down."

They make their way to the folding chairs. Neil sits straight up, in his presiding position. "Do you think it's easy to be a *man*? We're not even allowed the luxury of depression! We have to be *strong* all the time. We have to be *right* all the time. We have to be *leaders* all the time. And sometimes it's a real drag! Of course, there are fringe benefits. Men commit suicide three to four times more often than women, have a forty percent higher cancer rate, and a four hundred percent higher rate of heart disease. I think I would trade that for a little *depression!*"

Karen takes his hand, pauses, then speaks quietly, "You can have some of mine, Neil. I'll share."

Neil slumps back in his chair, not presiding. His fingers move gently over the back of Karen's hand. "Karen. Do we just have to live with all this?"

"I don't know how it happened, Neil. As far as I was concerned, life was going to be one long Gold and Green Ball."

"Yeah. You know what the first big blow was—to me?"

"What?"

"When you got pregnant. Oh, I wanted it. But you got

34

sick. You were not supposed to get sick. You were supposed to pop out twelve kids with hardly batting an eye. But you got sick. And you had to go to bed. It was like one month after I got married, my wife died."

Karen smiles. "The Gold and Green Ball came to a crashing halt."

"Children bring . . . so many changes. I wouldn't go back and *not* have them. I love them. But they make things . . . different."

Neil sighs and looks up at the still-turning celestial ball. Different! Oh, boy! Different! Take a simple thing like eating at the table. It used to be so . . . nice. So . . . simple. Just the two of them, talking about what happened that day and what would happen the next, talking even about philosophy or politics. And then—the highchair. It sort of . . . came between them. Soon they were serving up food for four. And the conversation changed. Radically. "What's this green stuff?" "I hate casseroles!" "Make her quit it!" "Jerry threw my coat out of the bus!" "He took my spoon and now there's germs all over it!" "What's this brown stuff?" There used to be an adult female voice at the table. And an adult male voice. And those voices used to have such nice, enjoyable, peaceful conversations. Where did they go? The highchair. Children's voices can be nice too. Sometimes. But they're different. Really different.

How can you hate somebody so much after you've loved them so much?" Brad's hand tightens around Janet's, and not with affection.

"If you hate her so much now—was it really love?"

"Yes, it was love!"

Janet studies him. He reminds her of last summer when she tried out for that melodrama—squinted eyes, flared nostrils, lots of teeth. Even the lines sound familiar.

"It was love, and now it's hate! Every time I look at her I want to punch her lights out."

Janet nods. "Both of them."

Brad glances at her in disgust. "That was so funny I forgot to laugh."

"Boy, it's a good thing you didn't get married, Brad. How would you explain all that violence to your six children?"

"Just be quiet and let me die." Brad turns from the dance floor. "Let's get some air."

He leads Janet out onto the patio. He can breathe a little better out here. It's a more decent world out here, where the moon and the stars are and *she* isn't.

"Dying of a broken heart doesn't work, Brad." Janet takes his hand and smiles at him. "I've tried it."

"It isn't fair! The whole earth ought to open up and swallow me! That would make me happy. Very, very, very happy."

Janet studies him again. She would cast him. If he were trying out for a melodrama, she would definitely cast him.

"Don't you hate Jay?"

"Of course I don't hate Jay."

36

"But you might end up an old maid. You're—" Brad looks around and reduces his voice to a whisper. "You're twenty-three years old."

"You're right. I'm getting to be what they call an 'unclaimed jewel.' "

"Aren't you worried?"

Janet leans up against the wooden railing. The rain was two days ago, but the wood still smells alive. Rain always does that—it makes dead wood smell alive again. And the smell of live wood always evokes those powerful yearnings. Do they go forward or backward? Are they memories or hopes? They're magic. They're elusive, but they press against her heart like the breath that is heavy with wood after rain. Was she worried? Is yearning worry?

She turns back to Brad. "Worried that nobody will ever claim me? No. I want to get married, have children. But I'm not going to sit around and wait for some guy to come along and validate my parking ticket. If I should never get married—which I do not think will happen— there are lots and lots of wonderfully interesting things to do."

"Did you really love Jay?"

Janet takes a deep breath and lets the yearnings go backward for a moment and become memories. "Yes. I loved him. You want to hear about it?"

"Sure. Misery loves company."

"Well. We were really good friends for about a year. You know that."

"Yeah. You used to come over all the time to do your homework."

"We had a Book of Mormon class together. Well, right

37

in the middle of Mosiah I fell in love with him. Only he didn't feel any differently at all. I was still just his good buddy, and I'd introduce him to my girl friends, and he'd tell me all about his romances. He didn't know how crazy I was about him. Finally he asked me to go to this dance, and I was so excited I thought I would die. We were dancing away and he whispered to me, 'Janet, do you believe in being a helpmeet?' 'Sure,' I whispered back. 'Sure, I do.' 'Great,' he said. 'How about helping me meet that girl over there in the green dress?' "

"What a bummer!"

"No." Janet smiles. "He was always honest with me. Later, when his feelings did change, he was honest about that too. He grew to love me. And he let me know."

"Janet, he *didn't* love you. He married somebody else."

"Brad, he *did* love me. And he married somebody else."

"That's crazy!"

"And true."

"Weren't you bitter?"

"For a while I was. Maybe a better word is—devastated. I was going to throw myself into the Great Salt Lake, but I was afraid I might not stay under. Then I was going to join a nunnery, but the bishop wouldn't write a letter for me. So I decided just to go right on living. And it worked. See? She breathes. She moves. She dances."

Brad shakes his head. "If he had loved you, it would have lasted."

"You are so young! There are many shades and grades of love. And they're all nice. We learned a lot from each other. We gave a lot to each other. I know he's happy. And I know I'm a better person because of him. We have

38

only good memories of each other. I wouldn't erase it if I could."

The memories. They came easily. They would have come easily even if the dead wood did not smell alive again. And with the wood she suddenly smelled gardenia. She closed her eyes and that wonderful night came back. They had shared many good times, but it was always that night that came first when she fingered the memories like beads. That night he had brought her a gardenia and a feeling she had never felt before—an incredible combination of being liked and loved, being esteemed and desired, being person and woman, being spirit and body in a whole new way—a way that she could only describe as glimpsing a new dimension, grasping a new meaning that made marvelous new sense. Words wouldn't take her much beyond that, because what was going on was clearly in the kingdom of the right brain, not the left. People call it being in love, of course. But you don't analyze it. You just feel it, know it. Like the smell of gardenia, it fills you and moves you. And like the smell of gardenia, it lingers—long after life is gone. That glimpse—can it ever come again? And stay . . . and widen? Gardenias bloom still.

Well, ladies and gentlemen, it's floor-show time."

The band gets a break. The dancers get a rest. And Howard gets the spotlight. Howard loves the spotlight. It's bright and it's warm and it makes him feel very much alive. More alive, in fact, than he feels at any other time.

"But first a few words from your friendly neighborhood MC. That's me, of course. Hey, listen! I have just come up with the most fantastic way to simplify genealogy—cut it right in half. Cloning. Great, huh?"

What did she mean, maybe he didn't really want to meet anybody? He was always friendly. Real friendly. He was the best MC around—they even called him from outside the stake, he had such a great personality. Look at them all, still laughing. That cloning joke was really a good one. It's a terrific feeling to have a couple of hundred people looking at you and smiling, laughing at your great jokes. He was really at home with a couple of hundred people. With a mike in his hand—or with a pulpit in front of him—life was like it ought to be and he could really shine, really give. But . . . take away the pulpit, take away the mike, take away the couple of hundred people, and leave—just one. One is not a very fun number. One does not laugh as loud. One does not generate that high energy, that great appreciation that a couple of hundred do. How do you perform for just—one? The dialogue gets dull. "What's your name?" "Where are you from?" "That's a nice dress." "Do you like the band?" He had solved the problem to a degree. He had learned how to take a real small audience, like . . . one . . . and sort of pad it, bring back a bit of the pulpit and the mike and the spotlight. Then things got more comfortable. Look at all those great people out there, laughing at him, loving him.

"I know that cloning sounds pretty boring, but maybe there's more to it than meets the eye. Maybe you could turn it into a truly meaningful relationship. Take yourself out to dinner first. Put on a little 'Music to Clone By,' something like 'Tea for One.' "

Howard breaks into a little soft-shoe and sings. " 'Picture me upon my knee—' Naaa! Guess I'll have to go on looking for my eternal mate. Say, a funny thing happened on my way to the dance tonight! I was. . . ."

A funny thing happens when the spotlight goes out, when the hall is cleared and there's nobody left but—one. After the show is done . . . a funny thing happens.

The audience is down to one now. Alison has properly admired Howard's great job as MC. But the spotlight is off now. The lights are dim, in fact.

"A nickel for your thoughts, Alison. Isn't it too bad what inflation's done?"

41

"My thoughts? Oh, nothing."

"You can't think nothing. It isn't possible. Tell me. I'd like to know what you're feeling about your life."

Alison's feet stop moving. She isn't supposed to stop. He's supposed to lead and she's supposed to follow. But she stops moving and looks at him.

"What I'm feeling? You want to know?"

Howard's feet stop moving too. "Yes. I do."

"Why?"

His feet start moving again. "I'm writing an article for the *Ensign*. 'Everything You Wanted to Know About a Mormon Divorceé but Were Too Polite to Ask.' Think they'll buy it?"

"Howard!" Alison grabs him by the shoulders and makes him stop and look at her. She shouldn't be talking that loud at the dance, almost yelling. And her face should not have that pained, angry look. "Howard—stop it! Don't you see what you're doing? Don't you see?"

Howard pauses, searches for the right comeback that will smooth everything over. Nothing. He takes her hand and leads her from the floor.

"I'm sorry, Alison. I never know when to quit, do I?"

"No. You don't."

"But I'd like to. Honest. Look—can we just talk? Somewhere, not here. Can we go out to my car?"

"Sure."

It's nice out in the car. The sound of the crickets and the sound of the band are about even. And the tapping of Howard's foot against the brake. After a moment he speaks.

"You want some gum?"

42

"No. No, thanks."

"Me neither." He puts it away. After massaging the steering wheel for a moment, he speaks again.

"You're right, you know, about . . . everything. About me. I guess I hide a lot—behind my jokes and stuff. But I don't want to. Not all the time. I'm sick of skin-deep relationships. When I think that I could get to the end of my life and never really know another human being—and that no one would ever know me—it terrifies me. That could happen."

"Don't let it."

"How? I don't know how."

Alison shrugs. "Let somebody in. Open up a little."

Howard massages the steering wheel again. "Show me."

"How?"

"Tell me about yourself. Tell me really."

"It isn't a funny story."

"I don't need a funny story. I don't *want* a funny story. Tell me."

"Where should I start?"

"With your marriage."

"Oh, you want the heavy stuff?"

"I guess I do."

Alison leans back, takes a deep breath, and rolls down the window. The sound of the band and the crickets is louder.

"My marriage. Well. I was nineteen, went right from my father's house to my husband's house. Two years of college, but I lived at home. The only real goal I had growing up was a temple marriage. That's as far as I had ever planned."

She closes her eyes. "To the temple by the river . . ." That wasn't the band. That was the trio at her wedding reception, all girls she had gone to high school with, girls that envied her being the first of them to marry, to become a real woman. She tunes out the trio and concentrates on the crickets.

"Dennis came along and everything went like clockwork." She looks over at Howard. "I loved him. I really did love him."

Howard nods. "Yeah."

"When we got married we moved into this little tiny basement apartment, so little that sometimes I'd get grease spatters on his term papers, the table was that close to the stove. He laughed about it—at first—said it was something to remember me by in his advanced business administration classes. Am I boring you?"

"No. No, go on."

"He was getting a master's. I worked as a typist, until the first baby came. We found a little bigger apartment, still in a basement. Very depressing places, basements are. I tried to fix it up with the things we made on homemaking day in Relief Society, but it was still depressing. There was no money to do anything with. No place for Dennis to study. And then the next baby came. 'Can't you keep those kids quiet?—I've got all this studying to do.' Of course I couldn't keep them quiet. So he'd leave and go to the library."

"The library. We all have our own little escapes, don't we?"

"One night I blew up. 'I wish I had a place to run to,' I said. 'I wish I could go to the library. You think I like being alone here with two children all day from morning until night except for a few hours at church, and they can't even go to the nursery because they're not toilet trained yet? You think that's my idea of a good time? I wish *I* could go to the library!' "

"What did he say?"

"Nothing. He just . . . went to the library. I shouldn't have said that. He wasn't having an easy time either. We had this great social relations lesson on seeing from the other person's point of view, walking in their moccasins. That helped me for a while. I wish he'd had the lesson too. Well. There were no more jokes about grease spatters on his term papers. There were no more jokes about anything. It's amazing how quickly you can lose your sense of humor in a basement. He stopped waking me up for a kiss when he came home late. I stopped making sure the tablecloth at dinner didn't have crumbs from lunch on it. You know. Maybe you don't know."

"I know."

"The sad part is that at the time I did not know what I could possibly do differently. But looking back I can see that wasn't true."

"Like what?"

"For instance, our Relief Society president was really a sharp lady. She arranged a baby-sitting pool one afternoon a week so that anybody who wanted to could go out and do anything they chose. Can you believe that I turned it down?"

"Why?"

"Everybody I know did. It would have been admitting defeat. 'If I can't take care of my own children, I'm not

45

going to ask someone else to do it for me.' Can you believe how stupid I was? Imagine the look on Dennis's face if ever he'd come home and I'd said, 'Guess what I did today? I climbed up to the "Y" on the mountain all by myself. Here's a rock I found for you—great paperweight!' But no. He'd come home and see me sighing and suffering. Is it getting boring yet?"

"No. Go on."

"It was to Dennis. Was to me too. Home was boring. Being together was boring. All he talked about was business trends. All I talked about was diapers and the children's teeth. Very boring."

Every once in a while Howard hears stories like this and it gets pretty discouraging. It's enough to make you want to stop searching for your eternal mate. What was the statement on that poster?—it had stuck with him like a scene from a scary movie. "The wagon of love breaks under the burden of life." Did it have to be that way?

Alison is still talking. "Even when he couldn't use the library as an excuse anymore, there was always something else. Church—soon he was in the bishopric. Community work—every good cause in town needed him. When he wasn't out doing church work, he was out saving the mountains and saving the river. Before long the bishop saw what was happening—talked to both of us, set up a counseling program. By then it was too late. While out saving the mountains and the river . . . Dennis had . . . met . . ."

Alison breaks off and turns her face toward the window. Howard reaches for her hand.

"She had a family too. When I found out, I went to stay with a friend for the weekend. I came back, and as soon as I opened the door, I knew. The record stand was empty. His guitar was gone. Everything of his was—gone."

"I'm sorry."

"You know what tomorrow is?"

"What?"

"My birthday. Today I got a card from him. Best wishes. He means it."

"It's been tough, hasn't it?"

"He was . . . my whole world."

The sound of crickets is healing. Sort of like the ocean. The sound of something that goes on and on and on puts you in touch somehow with permanence. And you feel safe for a moment, like you do as a child when you're in bed and you hear the clink of dishes in the kitchen and the sound of running water. Crickets just go on and on. "To the temple by the river . . ." Rivers go on and on too. Like other things are supposed to. "In the presence of God, angels, worlds without end, time and eternity." Eternity. Eternity was—almost nine years.

"I'm so glad when Daddy comes home—" When, oh, when will Daddy come home?

"No, no—Mama's not crying—"

"Jesus wants me for a sun—"

"If you chance to meet a—"

"School thy feelings, oh—"

"Yes, we're doing fine. I'll let you know if we need anything."

"Sing we now at . . . parting—"

"Till we meet at Jesus'—"

"Change it for a—"

Smile at the sisters. Give the closing prayer. Lie to the children why Daddy's not—

"There is beauty all—"

Around and around and around it goes. Where it stops nobody—

Nobody! That's what it comes down to. I am nobody. Without him I am nothing. Without him—

"I am . . . a child . . . of—"

God help me! I am *not* nobody! Before *him* I was somebody. And after him I am somebody. In the presence of God, angels, worlds without end, time and eternity—I am *me!*

Crickets. Oceans. God. There are things that continue on and on. There are!

They are walking around the block now. Alison's shoes aren't made for walking. But she'd much rather walk than dance right now. She puts her arm easily through Howard's. Touching someone is *lots* easier after you've told them something really important about yourself. They walk for a moment in silence.

"Okay, Alison. It's my turn. I may never again work up the nerve. But here goes . . . I . . . I . . . I can't do it."

"Sure you can. Tell me something you've never told anybody in your whole life."

Howard thinks for a moment, then speaks hurriedly before he changes his mind. "I have pimples on my back. Even when I go to the beach I keep a shirt on because I'm so embarrassed about it."

Alison smiles. "Now, that wasn't so hard, was it? Go on. Tell me something about your family. What were your mother and father like?"

"Nice people. Good people. Tried very hard to do what was right."

"Did they love each other?"

"Love? I suppose so. I have this very vivid picture in my mind of my dad on the couch with his arm around my mother. I think it's so vivid because it's the only time I remember seeing it. She had come home from the hospital that day. I guess they loved each other. They just didn't know how to show it. Nobody at our house really knew anybody else. The only conversation at the dinner table was about passing the salt and pepper and stuff like that."

"You see, Howard, you *can* talk about yourself. What else?"

"What else? I have this recurring dream. I have it a couple of times a month at least. I'm walking in this forest-like place, and I hear a baby cry. I keep walking and it gets louder and louder. And then, right there under this tree— I see my mother. Only she's a baby, a little tiny baby that's crying and crying. I don't know how I know it's my mother, but I know it is. I look around and I think, 'Why doesn't somebody pick this baby up?' But nobody's there except me. I reach down and pick up the baby, and I say, 'Hey, it's okay, it's okay!' And she stops crying. My mother stops crying. When I wake up I feel so dumb. But before I wake up—it's really beautiful, just holding her like that."

"That's a wonderful dream, Howard."

"And I cry in sad movies. I never take a date to a movie unless I know it's a comedy. I was double-dating once and they insisted on seeing 'Love Story.' Every time I felt it coming I'd go out for more popcorn. I was sick by the time it ended."

Talking faster makes you walk faster. "I cry in testimony meeting too. And one time the elders quorum fixed up and painted the house of a widow in the ward. As a surprise. She came home before she was supposed to and caught me painting her mailbox. She didn't say a word—just burst into tears. I didn't say a word either— just stood there with the paintbrush in my hand and tears rolling down my cheeks. Boy! Imagine telling somebody about that."

Alison squeezes his arm. "Howard, you're a very beautiful person."

He kicks a rock out of the path. "Thanks."

"Come on, let's get back to the dance."

"But I'm just getting warmed up."

"It'll keep. Listen, how about coming over to my house next Sunday evening, and you can pick up right where you left off."

"Sounds like a plan. Only, listen, Alison—I don't want

50

you to misunderstand, or start expecting anything. I'm just not ready to—"

Alison interrupts. "I am not asking you to marry me. I'm not interested in marrying anybody just now. I have to get to know myself all over again. Besides, I hear you have pimples on your back."

Howard looks at her, startled. Then, still walking, he gives her a kiss on the forehead. "Come on. Let's dance."

Brad pulls Janet toward the punch bowl, his nostrils flaring again. "Did you hear what she said to me? Did you?"

"No."

"When I had finished my dance, she wiggled up to me and said, 'Oh, Brad, that was marvelous. When you were out there dancing, a little voice inside me said—' "

"Oh, no!"

"Oh, yes!"

"What did you say?"

"I said, 'Marcie, would you go hide your light under a bushel?' "

Janet laughs and reaches for some punch. "Just give her a few years, Brad. Here's to Marcie at age twenty-three."

Brad lifts his cup. "Forget Marcie. Here's to me. I'm not gonna let a dumb girl run my life any more than those jerks at school. Look, everybody! Here's to *me*!"

Janet raises her cup. "To you."

"Hey! Do you still believe in being a helpmeet?"

Janet looks around. "Sure. Which one?"

"There's a real cute brunette with long straight hair right over there."

They put their cups down on the table. "Let's go."

Karen, you can't play 'The Newlyweds' at the seminar. The questions they ask are crazy."

It's difficult to hold an effective meeting while you're dancing. It requires concentration.

"Well, it might help bring out things that aren't usually brought out."

"Sure. Like knives . . . boxing gloves. 'Husbands, would you say that your wives would rather be in Relief Society, reading the Sunday paper, skiing, or taking a nap?' "

"Okay! Okay! Listen! How about—each person has to write down something their spouse did in the last month that made them happy and something that made them miserable? Then they read each other's."

Neil considers for a moment. "All right."

"Let's try it. Go ahead. Tell me."

"Well. Let's see. This is the good one. Last month when I had to spend the whole day in the garage working on the car—and I told you I couldn't even take the time to come in for lunch—I open the hood and there's a tuna sandwich taped to the engine. And a flower. I liked that. I really liked that."

Karen smiles. "That was fun."

"And the other one. Well, that time when we forgot about the Carlsons' party—and you made me tell them our baby sitter couldn't make it—"

"I was just so *embarrassed*."

"I know. But I felt terrible. And hurt."

"Yeah. I'm sorry. That was not fun. I'm sorry."

They dance in silence for a few moments. Then Neil looks at Karen expectantly. "Well? Your turn, Karen. Did I do anything in the last month to make you happy?"

"I'm thinking."

"*Six* months? How about a year?"

"Neil! Okay. I'm going to start with the other one. There was something—just last week—that really . . . hurt me."

"Go on."

Karen pauses. "Oh, boy! Why is it so much easier to fast and pray about a problem than to talk about it? Okay. I know it is not easy for you to be out in the world all day.

But it is also not easy for me to be home all day. And usually my hours are not filled with a whole lot of variety and excitement. True?"

"True."

"And so when I got the idea about taking that dance class, it sounded so great. It could help me keep in shape— I mean *get* in shape. And . . . well, twice a week when I could fix myself up a little and go out and think only about my body instead of somebody else's and listen only to music instead of to who needs what—and just let loose and move and go! It became a kind of a symbol—of something for *me*. So I told you about it that morning at breakfast."

"I remember."

"Here's our conversation. Me: 'So I would really, *really* like to try to figure out a way to do it. I know it's a little more expensive than just jogging, but—' You: 'So jog.' Me, with great patience: 'Neil, I know it sounds silly to you, but for some reason this is terribly important to me. It isn't just a dance class. It's symbolic of—something in my life. I've thought about it a lot. I've even fasted about it.' You: 'Fasting's a good way to lose weight. Just keep at it, fasting and jogging.' "

"I said that?"

"You said that. And you went to work. And I went into the bedroom. And cried."

"I'm sorry. I really am." Neil pulls her closer. "I think tomorrow we should go over our budget again. Anything that's that important to you—well, it's important."

"Okay."

"Have you thought up your *good* story yet? You can go back *two* years if you need to."

Karen laughs. "I don't need to."

"Whew!"

"Night before last, when Jeffrey was so sick—I had been up most of the night before—I was absolutely dead. Well, I woke up in the middle of the night, and you were not in bed. Then I heard you down the hall in Jeffrey's room, and you were saying, 'Now, let's be really quiet and not wake up Mommy. She has to have her sleep. We'll clean you up first, and then we're going to have a special get-well prayer, and then I'll lie down with you here for a little while.'"

"You heard all that, huh?"

"I just lay there and listened to you moving around and talking, and playing that guessing game, and singing 'Raindrops Keep Falling on My Head.' When you came back to bed I didn't let you know I was awake. And I couldn't go back to sleep for a while. I just lay there being happy, and really grateful that you were . . . you, and here, and with us."

Karen's cheek is soft against his. "Thanks."

"Neil. Why do you suppose that with everything Jesus said about love, he never once mentioned being *in* love?"

"I don't know."

"I wish he'd given a sermon on some mount called, 'Keeping Love Alive in Your Marriage.'"

"Maybe he did. 'Do unto others as you would have others do unto you.' Maybe that covers it."

Karen pulls away and looks at him. "Hey, that's not a bad title. 'A Newly Discovered Text by Jesus on Keeping

Love Alive in Marriage.' " She glances at her watch. "And we've got five minutes to spare."

The band is playing an oldie again. "Stardust." There is no vocalist, but the words come anyway. ". . . When our love was new, and each kiss an inspiration. But that was long ago, now my consolation. . . ." New things are wonderful. Old things can be too.

Neil gives her a gentle kiss. "Well, I sort of hate to admit it, but this has been quite a productive meeting."

Karen nods, silent.

"I've got it! Karen, you and I need more—meetings. Look, we get to all our meetings, don't we? We get to church meetings, school meetings, board meetings. Sure! We'll just put us on the schedule. When we want a date with each other, we won't call it that. We'll call it a *meeting*! And when we want to go to bed early, we'll call it a *meeting*! And we'll pass around the roll! And—damn it —we'll *get there*!"

Karen laughs, delighted. "Neil, I just remembered, I do have the spiritual thought. I love you."

"And I've got a faith-promoting story. A couple of weeks ago when I was working in the geriatrics ward, there was this little old lady dying of cancer. Every day at three in the afternoon her little old husband would toddle in, and then again at seven at night. They would mostly just sit and hold hands and smile at each other. One afternoon I arranged to be right there at 2:58 taking her pulse. He walked in the door—and it went up seven beats per minute, just like that. Seven beats is not off the chart, but it's *something*. Right there in geriatrics. Would you call that a faith-promoting story?"

Karen speaks in a whisper. "I would call that a faith-promoting story."

It's not easy to dance cheek-to-cheek when the music has changed to a wild, wild rhythm. But it can be done. It can be done.

The musicians pack their instruments. The round ball stops its celestial turning. The clouds and the silver stars and the rainbow streamers are left for the cleanup committee. The parking lot empties.

They have come to the dance. Male and female have left their lone and dreary worlds to spend a moment in the garden before the division. They have touched. They have remembered. They have yearned. They have discovered. They have seen things just a little differently than before. Even eros and agape have danced together. And gone home together.

The dancers take their steps in other directions. The music changes. And the dance goes on.